Contents

Any words appearing in the text in bold, **like this**, are explained in the glossary.

A plant may be called different things in different countries, so every type of plant has a Latin name that can be recognized anywhere in the world. Latin names are made of two words – the first is the genus (general group) a plant belongs to and the second is its species (specific) name. Latin plant names are given in brackets throughout this book.

What is growth?

As you stand beneath the arching branches of a mighty tree it is hard to imagine that it began life as a tiny **seed**, perhaps hundreds of years ago. All living things – plants and animals – grow and become bigger. Growth is a vital part of life.

When a plant begins its life, it is small and weak. One of the reasons it grows is to become stronger and bigger so that it is better able to obtain the things it needs to live and to survive any challenges that might come its way – from a fierce storm to a hungry **grazing animal**. The other reason living things grow is to become mature – an adult – ready or able to produce young like themselves that will live on after they have died.

The trees that time forgot!

Did you know that the oldest living things on Earth are trees? In California, USA, there is a bristlecone pine (*Pinus longaeva*) that is 4765 years old. It's amazing to think that Methuselah, as the tree is called, was a sapling (young tree) when the ancient Egyptians were busy building their pyramids!

▶ A bristlecone pine.

The Life of Plants

Plant Growth

Richard & Louise Spilsbury

Heinemann
LIBRARY

www.heinemann.co.uk
Visit our website to find out more information about **Heinemann Library** books.

To order:
 Phone 44 (0) 1865 888066
 Send a fax to 44 (0) 1865 314091
Visit the Heinemann Bookshop at www.heinemann.co.uk to browse our catalogue
and order online.

First published in Great Britain by Heinemann Library,
Halley Court, Jordan Hill, Oxford OX2 8EJ
part of Harcourt Education.
Heinemann is a registered trademark of Harcourt Education Ltd.

© Harcourt Education Ltd 2002
First published in paperback 2003
The moral right of the proprietor has been asserted.

Designed by Macwiz
Illustrations by Jeff Edwards
Originated by Ambassador Litho Ltd
Printed in China by Wing King Tong

ISBN 0 431 11881 7 (hardback)   ISBN 0 431 11888 4 (paperback)
06 05 04 03   07 06 05 04 03
10 9 8 7 6 5 4 3 2   10 9 8 7 6 5 4 3 2 1

British Library Cataloguing in Publication Data
Spilsbury, Louise
        Plant growth. – (Life of plants)
        1.Plants – Growth – Juvenile literature
        I.Title II.Spilsbury, Richard, 1963–
        571.8'2

Acknowledgements
The Publishers would like to thank the following for permission to reproduce photographs: Holt Studios: pp5, 6,
7, 8, 9, 10, 11, 12, 15, 16, 17, 19, 20, 23, 25, 29, 30, 32, 33, 34, 35, 36, 37, 39; NHPA: p22; Oxford Scientific Films: pp4,
13, 14, 18, 21, 24, 26, 27, 28, 31, 38; leaf motif: PhotoDisk

Cover photograph reproduced with permission of Oxford Scientific Films.

Our thanks to Andrew Solway for his comments in the preparation of this book.

Every effort has been made to contact copyright holders of any material reproduced in this book. Any omissions
will be rectified in subsequent printings if notice is given to the Publisher.

How quickly do plants grow?

We humans grow fastest as babies and very young children. After that we grow more slowly, except perhaps for a bit of a growth spurt when we are teenagers. When we reach adulthood, we stop growing. We get older and we may get fatter or thinner, but we do not grow any taller and our feet do not grow any longer. Plants, on the other hand, go on growing throughout their entire lives. Even when they have grown to maturity, many plants still go on growing.

And while most people grow at roughly the same rate, different plants grow at very different rates. Some plants grow quickly and others grow more slowly. A type of bamboo plant from Myanmar (Burma) has thick **stems** that can increase in height by up to 46 centimetres a day! The record for being the slowest-growing plant goes to a Mexican palm-like plant called *Dioon edule*. These plants may live for up to 3000 years, but often grow less than one centimetre taller each year!

► Bamboo plants like these in Columbia are one of the fastest-growing **species** of plants in the world.

How growth works

All living things — plants and animals — are made up of millions of tiny living parts called **cells**. Cells are the basic units of life, and different kinds of cells form the different parts of all **organisms** (living things). The size a living thing becomes is nothing to do with the size of its cells — cells are so incredibly tiny that they can usually only be seen through a microscope. The size of an individual depends on the number of cells that it contains.

Making more cells

In order to grow, living things need to increase the number of cells in their body. Most plants start life as a **seed**, made up of a certain number of cells. To grow into a new plant and increase in size the cells in the seed divide — each cell splits in two to create two cells. Then those two divide again, making four cells. The cells go on dividing like this, and as they increase in number, different groups of cells begin to specialize, developing into specific kinds of cells. These different kinds of cells form the different parts of the plant. Some kinds of cells form the leaves; others become the petals of a flower or the **roots** that grow under the ground.

◄ An oak tree is much bigger than a primrose because it has trillions more cells in each of the parts that make up its giant body.

What plants need to grow

The cells that make up every living thing – including you – need **energy** to live and increase their number. Humans and other animals get the energy they need from food, which they find, hunt or buy. Plants also need food to provide them with energy for growth, but they cannot move around to get it. Plants are able to make their own food, using a process called **photosynthesis**. The things they need to carry out this process are water, light and air.

To grow well, plants also need **nutrients**, space and the right temperature. But different plants require different amounts of all these things; too much or too little of any one may slow down or even stop a plant's growth. In this book we are going to find out how a plant uses its parts to get the right amounts of what it needs to make it grow, and what else it needs to make its growth successful.

Successful growth

Plants are the largest living things on Earth. Giant redwood trees (*Sequoiadendron giganteum*) can grow up to 2500 tonnes in weight. Blue whales are the largest creatures in the animal kingdom and even the biggest blue whale cannot compete with a giant redwood, weighing in at a mere 200 tonnes.

Starting to grow

Most plants start life as a **seed**. Seeds have a tough outer coat that protects the contents. Inside the seed there is an **embryo** (a tiny baby plant), which consists of a tiny **root** and a **shoot**. A seed is a bit like an egg with a baby chicken growing inside. Just like an egg, the seed contains a food store. This store of food keeps the embryo alive and fuels the start of growth in the seed – **germination**.

When the time is right

A plant makes seeds in its flowers. When the seeds are fully grown, the parent plant releases the seeds. Some of these seeds are eaten by animals and some land in places that are unsuitable for plant growth, but a few land in the right type of soil for the plant to grow. Some seeds germinate (start to grow) straight away, but many do not germinate for weeks, months or even years. The seed is able to survive until the conditions are just right. Most seeds need three things before they are able to germinate – water, air and warmth. In countries where a cold winter is followed by a warm spring, many seeds will not start to grow until the days begin to get warmer and there are more hours of daylight. These are the signals the seed needs to start to germinate.

▶ Most seeds are able to wait a long time until the conditions for germination are just right. This runner bean seed has a tough outer coat which protects the young plant inside.

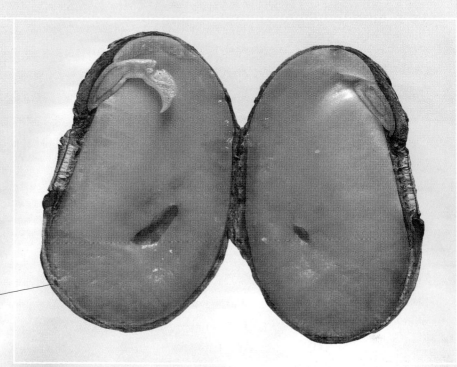

seed coat

Germination begins

While the seed lies in the soil, waiting for the right conditions for germination, it dries out a little. When germination begins, the seed soaks up lots of water from the soil around it. Inside the seed, the young root and shoot start to grow. As these grow they become too big for the seed and crack the seed's hard shell. The first sign of life is the young root. It forces its way out of one end of the seed and starts to grow down into the soil. The shoot is the next part of the plant to emerge. The young shoot with the plant's first **stem** and leaves pushes its way up, out of the top of the seed.

▲ Colourful flowers burst into life in Antelope Valley, California, USA.

A long wait

In some of the world's hottest deserts, rain may fall only once every few years. Seeds may have to wait a very long time until there is enough water for them to germinate. Seeds survive the dry periods underneath the ground. When the rains come, buried seeds suddenly burst into flower. It is as if someone has waved a magic wand. The empty desert is transformed into a sea of colour. This magnificent spectacle lasts only a few days or weeks. Then the harsh sun dries up the flowers and the plants die, leaving only the sand once more.

Roots and shoots

The **root** is the first part of the plant to start growing. After it has emerged from the broken **seed** case, it grows straight down into the soil. Roots almost always grow downwards because they respond to the pull of **gravity**, the force that makes things fall to the ground when we drop them. Even if a seed lands in the soil the wrong way up or there is a stone in the way, the root will wind around until it can grow downwards.

Different plants grow different kinds of roots. In some plants, such as carrots, there is one main root, which becomes quite thick and long. Smaller, thinner roots grow from this main root, branching out to the sides. Other plants, such as leeks, may have many roots of roughly the same size. All roots are strong, however small they may be. As roots burrow deeper into the soil, they bump into stones and other obstacles, such as other roots. Outer layers of the cap (tip) of the root rub off to help the root move more smoothly through the soil.

◄ **One of the jobs that roots do is to anchor the plant in the soil. Roots give the plant a firm grip on the ground so the shoot can start growing up.**

Going up – shoots

After the root has started to grow, the shoot begins to break out of the seed case too. Shoots grow in the opposite direction to roots – they always grow upwards, towards the light. The tip of the shoot is able to detect light so the plant knows in which direction to grow.

The shoot pushes its way up until it emerges above the soil. If you look carefully at the shoots of very young plants, you may be able to see the seed cases still attached to the top of the shoot. Once the shoot is in the light, it straightens up and the first leaves are revealed. As the leaves grow, the seed case falls off and drops to the ground where, having completed its task, it rots away.

When germination is complete

The early growth of the roots and shoot is fuelled by the food stored in the seed. In some seeds the food store is kept in the tiny leaves on the shoot. These are known as seed leaves. In others, it is stored around the **embryo**. Once the plant has established a root system and has grown its first true leaves – leaves that look like the leaves on the parent plant – **germination** is properly complete and the young plant now has the things that it needs to make food for itself.

▲ The narrow leaves at the bottom of this corn poppy are its seed leaves. They provide food for the seed to germinate. Once the plant's true leaves, nearer the top, have formed, the seed leaves die as they are no longer needed.

11

Getting water

Water is essential for all living things. Believe it or not you (and other animals) are made up of mostly water, which is in the **cells** that make up your body. Water accounts for around 95 per cent of the weight of a plant and many smaller plants rely on the water inside them to hold them upright. Plants not only depend on water to form their parts; they also need water to be able to make their own food in the process of **photosynthesis**.

Plants take in water through their **roots**. Plants that grow in ponds or lakes have a continuous supply of water all around them. Plants that grow on the land take in water from the soil. If the soil where a plant grows is very dry, its roots may have to grow very deep in order to find enough moisture. In woodland that is full of trees with deep roots, other plants may grow roots just below the surface of the soil. That way they can gather rainwater as it falls, before it soaks away into deeper ground.

◄ Smaller plants can survive amongst the roots of bigger trees because they have shallow root systems that can soak up rainwater before it drains down to the large, greedy tree roots below.

Root hairs

Water is sucked into a plant by the tiny root hairs that grow at the ends of its smaller roots. Root hairs on many plants are so small and thin that it is tricky to see them without the help of a magnifying glass. It is the fact that root hairs are so little that makes them so good at their job. They can grow around the fragments of stones and soil to find the water that is trapped between them. Also, there are so many root hairs that they greatly increase the plant's ability to take in water from the soil. After the root hairs collect the water, it is passed on to the smaller roots. From these the water travels into the main roots and finally up into the **stem** of the plant or trunk of a tree and on into its leaves.

World's deepest roots

At Echo Caves in Transvaal, South Africa, water is often scarce. In its desperate search for more water, a determined wild fig tree grew roots that extended 120 metres (400 feet) into the earth. That is about as deep as a 24-storey building is tall!

◄ The root on this radish seedling is covered in white root hairs. Each hair helps the plant take in more water from the soil.

Getting nutrients

Although plants can make their own food by **photosynthesis**, they also need other substances to help them grow and thrive. We call these substances **nutrients**, because they nourish the plant. Most plants take in nutrients from soil.

What is soil?

Soil is a mixture of tiny pieces of rock and the remains of decayed plants and animals. It is formed when rocks are gradually broken up by wind and rain. As decayed leaves and dead plants and animals rot away they are washed into the ground and also become part of the soil. So soil contains nutrients from decayed living things and **minerals** from rock fragments.

Nutrients in water

Many of these nutrients and minerals are **dissolved** in water that is found in soil. Plants take in these nutrients and minerals when they take in water through their **roots**. Water travels up from the roots through the rest of the plant in a set of tubes called **xylem**. Xylem in a plant are rather like the pipes in a house, transporting water from one part to another.

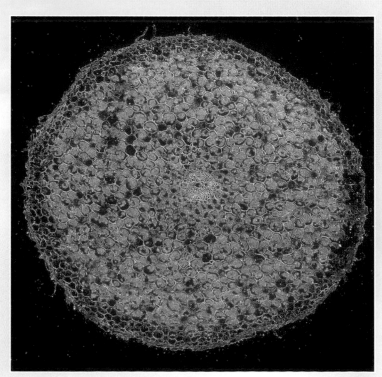

▶ This magnified picture of the inside of a root shows the xylem tubes that run through the whole plant.

Transpiration – taking in water

The way plants take in water is a bit like the way you drink with a straw. As water leaves the top of a straw (when it is sucked into your mouth), more water fills the space left at the bottom of the straw. In plants, water travels through xylem tubes in the leaves. As water is lost from these tubes at the top of the plant, more water comes into the bottom of the tubes (in the roots) to replace it. The process is called **transpiration**.

Water escapes from the leaves because it **evaporates** and passes out of little holes on a leaf's surface, called **stomata**. This is how it works. As the sun warms the leaves, the water inside them heats up too. This makes some of the water evaporate – it turns into an invisible gas called **water vapour** and passes out of the stomata into the air. It's a bit like the way a T-shirt dries on a line. As the air warms the fabric, water within it evaporates, leaving your T-shirt dry.

Thirsty trees!

On a warm day a tree takes in about 1130 litres of water – enough to fill five baths! It takes in this much to replace water that it loses through its many leaves.

► As water vapour released from rainforest trees cools in the air it changes back into droplets of water, forming dense clouds.

Getting light

If you move a houseplant from a sunny windowsill to a dark cupboard, it will soon become pale and weak and eventually it will die. Plants cannot survive without some light – they need it to live and to grow. Plants collect light through their leaves and they have different ways of making sure their leaves are in the best positions to receive light.

For some plants it is a question of timing. Flowering plants that live on a woodland floor grow new leaves early in the spring. That way they get the light they need to produce flowers before the trees fill out with leaves and block the precious rays. Trees have tall **stems**, called trunks, supporting their branches. Their leaves grow from twigs on branches, which spread out like arms to hold the leaves out into the daylight. Branches in the **canopy** (upper part) of a tree grow so that their leaves do not overlap and block light from others.

Some plants use other ways to hold their leaves up to the light. Bladderwrack (*Fucus vesiculosis*) is a kind of seaweed. It has balloons of air within its leaves that make the leaves float near the water's surface, where there is most light.

◄ **The branches on this tree grow so that their leaves do not stop the light from reaching other leaves – making the canopy look rather like a giant green jigsaw puzzle.**

Cheats!

Epiphytes are the cheats of the plant world. They include plants, such as **algae** and **mosses**, which reach the light without the bother of growing long stems. Tropical orchids are epiphytes. Wind carries their tiny **seeds** onto tall trees. When they **germinate**, they grow some **roots** that clasp onto the tree and others that dangle in the steamy air to absorb water and **nutrients**.

▶ **Epiphytes are often called 'air plants' because of their lack of ground roots.**

Light and shade

Most leaves need a certain amount of light. If there is not enough, a leaf will not be able to make enough food to survive. If there is too much light, it can damage the parts within the leaf that make the plant's food.

All leaves have an outer layer called a **cuticle**. The cuticle is usually **waxy** and it helps to protect the fragile inner parts of the leaf. On leaves of plants such as ferns, which live in shade, it is thinner. This allows the leaves to absorb as much light as they can. Plants growing in bright sunlight have a thicker cuticle. Some sunlight still gets through, but the cuticle protects the leaf from the strongest rays. In hot places, some leaves also have little hairs growing on them. These help to filter (break up) the sunlight's harsh rays.

Leaves

Leaves are often called the plant's food factory. This is because food is made inside the leaves by a process called **photosynthesis**. Just like any other factory, work cannot begin until all the raw materials are in place. The raw materials that a leaf factory needs to make food are water and **carbon dioxide**, a gas in the air.

Water deliveries

Plants take in water through their **roots**, so how do they transport it all the way up to their leaves? The answer is that within the roots, **stems** and leaves of a plant there is a network of water-carrying tubes called **xylem**. The water moves from the roots to the stem and on into the leaves through these **xylem** tubes.

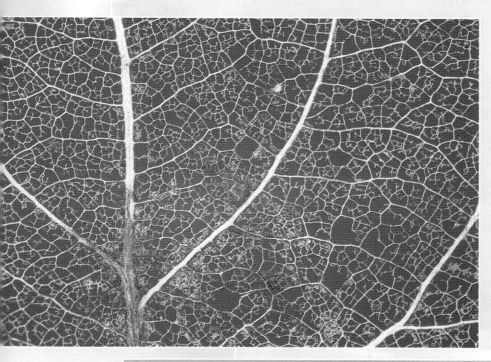

◄ This is a leaf skeleton. The softer green part has rotted away, leaving only the tougher veins of the leaf. These veins are tiny tubes, some of which are used to transport water all through the leaves.

What is a vascular plant?

Plants that have tubes in their roots, leaves and stems to transport water are called **vascular plants**. Vascular means 'having vessels' and a vessel is a tube or pipe that carries a fluid. Most of the plants in the world are vascular. Some plants, such as **mosses**, are different. All the parts of these plants can absorb water and **nutrients** so they do not need tubes to transport them.

Collecting carbon dioxide

Plants take carbon dioxide straight from the air into their leaves through tiny openings called **stomata**. Leaves have hundreds of stomata, but they are so tiny that you cannot usually see them. In some plants, most of the stomata are on the underside of the leaf. In others, there are stomata both on the top and on the underside of the leaf.

The stomata are also the holes through which **water vapour** escapes in **transpiration**. They can open and close to stop the leaf losing more water. Each hole is flanked by two guard **cells**, which open the stomata when they bend outwards and close it when they bend inwards. Most plants open their stomata during daylight hours, when photosynthesis usually occurs, and close them at night.

Talking to plants?

Do you know that some people believe talking to plants helps them grow? This may not be as crazy as it sounds. When you breathe out you release carbon dioxide from your body into the air. When you speak to a plant, you breathe this carbon dioxide towards its leaves. As plants need this gas to make food, perhaps chatting to them isn't such a bad idea after all!

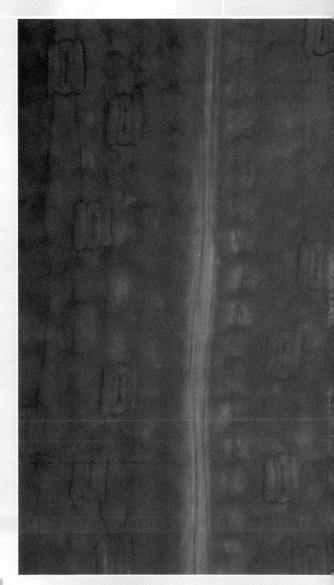

▲ This magnified picture of part of a leaf shows its stomata. You can see the two curved guard cells, which open and close the stomata, on either side of the holes.

Making food

Once the raw materials – the **carbon dioxide** and water – are in place, the leaf factory is ready to start work on food production. There is just one thing missing – like all factories the leaf needs a source of power. While an ordinary factory uses gas or electricity, the power source for **photosynthesis** is sunlight, which the plant absorbs through its leaves.

Light-trap

Daylight is essential to the process of photosynthesis. In fact the word 'photosynthesis' means 'putting together with light'. The leaf traps light using a remarkable **pigment** called **chlorophyll**. Chlorophyll is green and it is what gives leaves their green colour. You may have noticed that leaves are usually a darker green on the topside than on the underside. That is because there is more chlorophyll on the top of the leaf, where most of the sunlight falls. Even leaves that do not look green, like the red leaves of a copper beech tree (*Fagus cuprea*), contain chlorophyll. You just cannot see it because in certain plants other colours hide the green.

► **Photosynthesis occurs near the top surface of a leaf, where the sunlight is at its strongest. That is why most of the leaf's chlorophyll is concentrated in the top surface, making the upper part of a leaf look far greener than the bottom.**

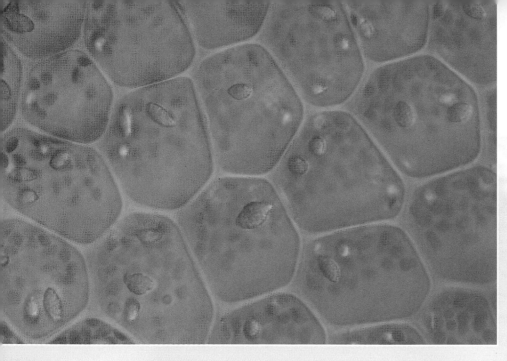

◄ The little green blobs you can see in this picture of Canadian pond weed cells are chloroplasts. The cells have been magnified about 200 times so you can see them.

Chlorophyll is made in tiny compartments called **chloroplasts**, within each leaf **cell**. The food-making cells within the leaves are packed with these chloroplasts. Chloroplasts use their chlorophyll to absorb sunlight. Then they use the sunlight's **energy** to combine the carbon dioxide and water to make food in the form of sugars.

Gas works

Inside droplets of water there are two different kinds of gas – hydrogen and **oxygen**. The leaf splits the water into these separate parts. Then, the hydrogen is combined with the carbon dioxide to form sugars. The plant uses some of the oxygen that is left and releases the rest into the air through the **stomata** (tiny openings) on its leaves. Now the plant can use the sugars – its 'food' – to fuel its own growth.

Photosynthesis and us

Photosynthesis is one of the most important things in the world. Without it not only plants would die, but we would too! During photosynthesis, plants release oxygen through their stomata. This oxygen is a vital part of the air that we breathe. This means that plants are vital for our survival in two ways. They are the source of all our food – when we eat them, or when we eat animals that eat plants. Also, if all the plants in the world died out, animals like us would soon use up the supply of oxygen that was left and die.

21

Using food

The food or sugars made by the plant in **photosynthesis** move out of the leaf in tubes called **phloem**. The phloem tubes contain water, which mixes with the sugars to form a sweet liquid called **sap**. The sap flows along the phloem tubes from the leaf, through the **stem** and on to all the other parts of the plant.

Storing food

The plant uses some of the sugars straight away, to provide the **energy** it needs to grow, and stores the rest. Most plants change extra sugars into starches, another type of food. Starch is easier for the plant to store than sugar. Some starches are stored in underground plant parts, such as a **root** or an underground stem. Potatoes and carrots are underground food stores. The reason we eat vegetables like carrots and potatoes is that we can also use the stored food for ourselves. The plant can turn the starch back into sugar when it needs more energy, such as when it is time to grow flowers and make **seeds**.

The syrup tree

The maple syrup you pour over a pancake is actually the sap of the sugar maple tree (*Acer saccharum*). Farmers drill holes into the wood until they reach the phloem and collect some of the sap that flows out. The sap is clear and slightly sweet and has to be boiled down to make the thick, sweet syrup that we buy.

Turning food into energy

A car engine gets the energy it needs to move from fuel. Plants and animals get the energy they need to live and grow from food. When an engine uses petrol, it has to burn it with **oxygen** to produce energy. When plants and animals make energy from their food, they use oxygen in a similar way.

Respiration

The process by which living things use oxygen to release energy from their food is called **respiration**. Some people think that respiration means breathing. In fact, breathing is just what animals do to get oxygen into their bodies and **carbon dioxide** out. Plants have three ways of obtaining the oxygen they need. They create an oxygen supply for themselves during photosynthesis, they take in oxygen through the **stomata** in their leaves, and they absorb oxygen through their roots (during **transpiration**) from tiny pockets of air in the soil.

In respiration, plants mix the oxygen with sugars within their **cells**. This special mixing releases energy. The cells can then use this energy to divide and increase their number in order for the plants to grow, and also to repair themselves when damaged. Along with energy, respiration also produces carbon dioxide, a gas which plants can use in photosynthesis.

▲ When it is time to grow flowers and produce seeds, plants convert some of the food made in photosynthesis to fuel the new growth.

Feeding on others

One group of plants does not use **photosynthesis** to make food. These plants are the burglars of the plant world because they survive by stealing food from other plants. They are called **parasites** and the plants that they feed off are known as 'hosts', even though the plants that feed on them are anything but welcome guests.

▶ **The giant rafflesia (*Rafflesia arnoldii*) is one of the most impressive parasites in the world. A single flower can weigh up to 7 kg and grow up to 1 m wide. Its host is a vine, which runs along the ground in the rainforests of South-east Asia.**

Many parasitic plants live in the shade because they do not need the sunlight for photosynthesis. Many do not have green leaves for the same reason. Some do not even have **roots** in the ground like other plants. They use their roots to attach themselves to other plants and to penetrate their **stems** and take the food that flows through the tubes – the **xylem** and **phloem** – inside. Other parasitic plants have roots in the soil, and they attach themselves to host plants by suckers, which grow out of their stem and into the other plant's stem. Some parasitic plants take so much food from the host plant that they starve it. Others seem to be able to take all the **nutrients** they need without destroying their host.

Dodder

The dodder (*Cuscuta*) is a good example of a parasite that attaches itself to a host plant using its stems. Dodder plants have string-like **tendrils** (long, very thin leaves) that stretch across the ground. If they reach a plant that is too thin or weak, they ignore it. When they reach a healthy plant, they wrap themselves around its stem and grip on tightly with suckers. The suckers pierce the stem and find their way into the host's food vessels. Using food from its host, the dodder is then able to grow very quickly until it almost covers the host plant. Then it carries on in search of another victim.

Mistletoe

Mistletoe plants (*Viscum album*) attach themselves to other plants using their roots. Adult mistletoe plants produce white berries that birds feed on. These are so sticky that to get rid of the **seed** after eating the fruit, the bird rubs its beak onto branches or cracks in tree bark. Thus settled, the seed grows a root which forces itself into the cracks of the branch and into the tubes that carry the tree's **sap**. It then sucks up this food for its own use.

◄ Mistletoe plants feed off a tree's food supply, but they have green leaves so they also make some of their food by photosynthesis. Plants like this are known as partial parasites.

Insect-eating plants

Most plants in the world have to cope with being eaten by insects, greedy for the food stored in their leaves or **roots**, or carried in their **stems**. Some plants, however, eat insects instead!

▲ This North American pitcher plant (*Sarracenia leucophylla*) has a kind of lid above the top of the pitcher to stop rain getting in.

Although they make their own food by **photosynthesis**, most insect-eating plants live in sandy, rocky or boggy soils that are not very rich in **nutrients**. Plants catch insects to get the extra nutrients they need for healthy growth. Usually, they trap the insects in some way and then use special juices to **dissolve** them – the juices break the insects down into smaller and smaller pieces until they become liquid. This liquid then passes easily into the plant.

Pitcher plants (*Nepenthes*) are some of the best-known insect-eaters. There are many different kinds, but they all entice insects with sweet-smelling **nectar**. Pitcher plants have special, tube-shaped leaves, which look like green jugs or 'pitchers'. When the insects enter the pitcher, they lose their grip and fall to the bottom. The sides of the pitcher are slippery so it is impossible for them to crawl out. They splash down into a pool of liquid at the bottom of the pitcher and quickly drown. The insect gradually dissolves and is absorbed into the plant's system.

Sundews

Round-leafed sundews (*Drosera rotundifolia*) live in **peat bogs**. They supplement their diet by catching insects, trapping them on sticky hairs that are on their long, curly leaves. At the end of each hair is a drop of sticky liquid. The liquid has a smell that attracts insects. When an insect lands on one of the hairs, it gets stuck in the liquid. Its struggles cause neighbouring hairs to curl around the insect. These hairs hold the insect tight while the plant's juices break down and dissolve it. The plant then absorbs the juices and makes use of the nutrients they provide.

A plant that can count?

At the end of the Venus flytrap's (*Dionaea muscipula*) narrow green leaves are two flat, rounded lobes. These offer insects a landing pad to rest on while they drink nectar there, which is advertised by a patch of red. In fact the lobes form a deadly trap, but to stop it springing shut for no good reason, say when a raindrop falls on it, the plant counts! Each lobe has a few hairs. If a fly touches only one of these hairs, it will be OK. If it touches two or more, the trap snaps shut and the spikes on the edges of the leaves interlock to form a cage. The teeth of these green jaws stay closed as the plant juices digest the fly.

Staying healthy

Plants need healthy parts to be able to grow well, but they often find themselves under attack. Insects use their sucking mouthparts to puncture the **stems** of plants to get at the sugary **sap** that flows within. Animals such as rabbits and deer eat their leaves and **roots**. In order to protect themselves against the insects and animals that regularly try to feed on them, some plants have defence systems – ways of protecting themselves.

Plant defences

Plants use spikes, thorns, stings, poison and even water traps to put off their enemies. Some plants are able to deter tiny insects with a set of fine hairs across their leaves. This makes it difficult for smaller insects to land or walk on the leaves. The thorns on the stem of a rose (*Rosa*) can be very painful for **grazing animals**, so they soon learn to leave it well alone. Some holly (*Ilex*) leaves are edged with curled prickles, which soon put off any would-be diners.

▶ On a teasel plant (*Dipsacus*) the leaves grow in pairs and where they meet at the stem a cup-shaped pool forms. This fills with rainwater and when insects and small snails climb onto the leaves to eat them, many slide into this pool and drown!

Bracken's lethal weapon

Bracken (*Pteridium aquilinum*) covers hillsides in almost every continent of the world, except Antarctica. One of the reasons a bracken plant is so successful is that it protects itself with deadly poisons that are released only when its leaves are chewed by animals. Large bracken plants make enough of these poisons to cause blindness or even cancer in grazing animals, such as rabbits and deer. Animals soon learn to steer clear of bracken, leaving the plant free to grow and spread far and wide.

How do stinging nettles sting?

Have you ever been stung by stinging nettles (*Urtica dioica*)? It hurts so much that most of us do our best to avoid them if we can. Imagine how that sting feels to a smaller animal, like a rabbit, and how efficiently it must put them off trying to eat the nettle's lush green leaves. How does it work? Stinging nettle leaves and stems are covered with tiny hairs that have sharp, pointed ends. The tip of these hairs can be broken off by even the gentlest touch. The broken edges are so sharp that they cut the skin of whatever animal touches the plant. At the same time, a poison stored in the base of the hair is released and squirted into the wound.

▲ The poisonous needles on a stinging nettle stem.

Helping plants grow

When gardeners or farmers grow plants for pleasure or to sell, they use their knowledge of what plants need to help them produce bigger and better plants. They can also grow plants from other countries and climates by giving them what they need artificially.

All plants need water, but farmers can grow plants in very dry soils by pumping water into the ground. This is called **irrigation**. Farmers also add **fertilizers** to soil. Fertilizers are **nutrients** that help to increase the amount and quality of the crops. People also put 'plant food' onto houseplants. This is a kind of fertilizer as well. As they grow, houseplants use up all the nutrients that are in the pot's soil, so people add plant food to replace the nutrients.

Gardeners and farmers often use greenhouses and plastic tunnels to provide plants with artificial warmth and shelter. The extra warmth helps the seeds to **germinate** and the plants grow better than they would if they had been planted directly outside. Some plants are kept in artificial conditions all the time. Hothouses, like those in botanical gardens, have heaters so people can grow heat-loving exotic plants like huge cacti and tropical flowers.

► Plant producers can control the time plants flower so they are ready exactly when consumers want them. These poinsettias (*Euphorbia pulcherrima*) are ready for Christmas.

Hydroponics

Hydroponics is a way of growing plants without soil. Instead, scientists grow plants in containers of water or small stones, such as coarse sand or gravel. They ensure the plants get everything they would normally get from soil: water, air and nutrients.

Plants grown in water do not have anything for their **roots** to hold on to, so they grow through a wire mesh, which holds them up. Their roots hang down, taking in water, which has nutrients added to it. Plants growing in soil also take in **oxygen** from the ground, so oxygen is pumped into the water for the plant to use.

Plants grown in containers of coarse sand or gravel can use their roots to anchor themselves, so they do not need any support. The grains of sand or gravel have air between them, but no nutrients or water. Water that contains nutrients is pumped up from below or sprinkled on these containers from above.

Growing plants by hydroponics does not make the plants bigger or better, but it is a useful way of finding out what plants need to grow well. Scientists can change the amounts or kinds of nutrients they give particular plants to see what produces the most successful growth.

▼ **Hydroponics is a good way to learn what plants need and it also proves that they do not necessarily need soil to grow!**

Ways of growing

Once a plant gets everything it needs, it can grow well, but exactly how does it grow and do plants grow more in some of their parts than in others?

At the tip

In many plants, growth is concentrated at certain points. Most growth occurs at the very top or bottom of a plant, such as the tips of leaves, twigs or **roots**. When leaves and **stems** grow longer and roots reach deeper into the soil, most of the plant's growth is happening just behind the tips or ends of the plant parts. For example, in a root the main growing point is at the very tip of the root. There, **cells** divide and increase in number to make the root increase in length. Some other plants, such as grasses, grow from their base instead.

Growing in buds

Safely hidden within protective **buds**, tiny flowers or young leaves start to grow. Petals grow curled up tight inside flower buds, and small, pale green leaves grow inside leaf buds. The buds keep them safe from cold and wind. Many buds only burst open in the spring or summer when the weather is warm enough for the young leaves and flowers to thrive.

▶ Unlike most plants, grass grows from the base not the tips of its leaves. This makes it an ideal plant for a lawn because it can recover quickly after being mown.

Tree growth

Trees grow in two different ways at the same time. As with other plants, they grow taller and deeper by growing at the tips of their twigs and roots. The trunk grows taller from the top and the roots grow longer. This means that when a branch grows out sideways from a trunk, it will always be the same height above the ground.

Trees, trunks, branches, twigs and roots can also grow fatter. All of these parts are covered in bark. Just below the bark is an area of growth called the **cambium**. When cells here divide, the parts of the tree get fatter. It is important for trees to grow wide trunks, because they need to be very strong to support their many, heavy branches.

▲ If you look at a section of trunk, you can see lots of **annual rings**. These are formed when the cambium grows outwards each year. By counting the annual rings you can find out the age of a tree.

World's fattest tree

The widest tree ever known grew in Sicily, Italy and reached its greatest size in the late 18th century. This European chestnut tree (*Castanea sativa*) was given the grand nickname 'Tree of 100 horses' because it measured a mighty 57.9 metres (190 feet) in circumference. It is still alive today, but it has split into three parts.

Growth shapes

Each **species** (type) of plant in the world grows in a typical shape. Although one sunflower is slightly different from another, they all have a tall **stem** with a large yellow flower head at the top. While one Norway spruce (*Picea abies*) may be taller and have more branches than another, they all have the same characteristic triangular shape.

Tree forms

The shape of each plant species is suited to the kind of **habitat** the plant usually lives in. For example, there is a reason why Norway spruces are triangular. They usually grow in cold places and are often covered in snow in winter. Their shape, with branches angled towards the ground, means much of the snow slides off their needles. Now think of a **deciduous** tree like a beech (*Fagus*) or maple (*Acer*). As it loses its leaves in winter it does not have to protect them from snow. However, it usually lives in woodland where there are lots of other trees. So, it has long branches that grow up and out to make sure its leaves get enough light for **photosynthesis** to occur.

◄ If the branches of this spruce tree spread out instead of down, the weight of heavy winter snows could seriously damage them.

Responding to the environment

Although all plant species try to grow in their characteristic shape, an individual plant grows to a shape that is affected by the environment in which it lives.

The amount of light, **nutrients**, water, space and heat a plant gets all affect how it grows. A bean plant grown in a shady spot is likely to be much paler and weaker than one grown in sunlight. If a **seed germinates** in soil without the right nutrients, the young plant may become unhealthy and develop blotchy leaves or weak stems. An ivy plant (*Hedera helix*) will grow to the shape and height of the wall it is using to support itself. On windswept coastal paths you may have seen trees such as blackthorn (*Prunus spinosa*) that would normally grow upright, growing hunched up and stunted. They have not usually blown over; instead, they have grown less on the side facing the wind, so that they bend away from the wind.

Straight and tall

Coniferous trees planted very close to others in plantations have to compete for space to grow and light for photosynthesis. So, they grow tall and straight with branches and needles only right at their tops. This means that when they are cut down, their trunks can be sawn into long, straight planks of wood with few knots (marks where branches have grown from the trunk).

◀ Strong winds blowing from left to right have stunted growth on the left side of this tree, making it look like it is blowing over.

Growth cycles

The human growth cycle usually goes like this — we are born, we grow from children to adults, when we may have children of our own, then we grow old and finally we die. The growth cycle is similar for plants — they grow, make flowers and **seeds** and then they die.

▲ The sunflower grows, flowers and dies in the same year, leaving its many seeds to survive and grow into new plants the next year.

Annual plants grow from seed, flower, spread seeds that can survive until the next growing season and then die, all in less than one year. Annual plants include flowering plants such as sunflowers (*Helianthus*) and poppies (*Papaver*).

Biennial plants take two years to complete their life cycle. In the first year they grow green leafy parts, which die back in the autumn. The plants store food, usually in their **roots**, to fuel growth in the following spring. In this second year biennial plants, such as wild carrots and foxgloves (*Digitalis*), produce their flowers and seeds, and then die.

Perennial plants, like trees and shrubs, live for two or more years, and most produce flowers every year. Many lose their leaves or even all their parts above ground in winter or a dry season. The roots store food so as to fuel new growth the following year.

Seasons

In the northern countries of the world the growth cycles of most plants are determined by the seasons. In spring, seeds **germinate**, new plants develop and established plants begin to grow again after resting throughout winter. In the hot summer months, plants flower and begin to produce fruits. In autumn the fruits ripen and die, releasing the plants' seeds.

In winter the days are shorter and there is less light for plants to use for **photosynthesis**. The freezing weather could destroy plant parts, such as leaves, so many **deciduous** trees shed their leaves and stop growing during the winter. They keep alive using food stored in their roots until spring comes when they grow new leaves and make their own food again.

Why do leaves change colour?

Leaves contain many colours, but in spring and summer the green **chlorophyll** hides them. In autumn trees stop producing new chlorophyll in the leaves and the old chlorophyll breaks down, letting other leaf colours – yellows, oranges, reds and browns – show through. This colourful display does not last long. The trees grow a layer of **cork** across the leaf stalks, plugging the pipelines that carry water. The leaves dry out, die and fall.

When a plant dies

The length of time an animal lives varies between different **species**. Few humans live for more than 100 years, while wolves live about 15 years, mice about 4 years and fruit flies only a few months. Different plants also have different life spans, ranging from a few months to hundreds of years. Plants, like animals, may also die before their time. **Grazing animals** may eat them or trample on them. **Parasite** plants may rob them of so much food that they starve. Sometimes humans cut plants down, to clear land.

The importance of recycling

Even when a plant is dead it still has a useful job to do. We all know how important it is to recycle as much as we can, whether it be glass bottles, newspapers or plastics. When a plant dies, it is recycled too. When plants, and animals, die, they begin to decay (rot). Small animals and insects eat parts of them, and what is left **decomposes** (breaks down into smaller and smaller pieces) until it is washed into the soil by rainwater. The **nutrients** and goodness that were in the plants now become part of the soil. New plants use the nutrients to help them grow, and the cycle of life, death and decay begins again.

▶ **Holes in dead trees make perfect hideaways for woodland creatures, like this northern flicker (Colaptes auratus).**

The death and decay of a tree

A dead tree may take as long as fifteen years to decay. A multitude of living things gradually break it down and help to release its nutrients back into the soil. Creatures such as millipedes and slugs eat dead leaves, releasing some of their goodness into the soil when it passes through the animals' bodies. Gradually the bark of the tree becomes loose and bits fall off, exposing the wood. This makes it easier for other insects and animals to eat or break into. Once the middle of the tree is rotten, the trunk is easily broken by wind and falls to the ground. Here **fungi** and **bacteria** get to work, turning the tree into a soggy pulp. Gradually all visible remains of the tree are gone.

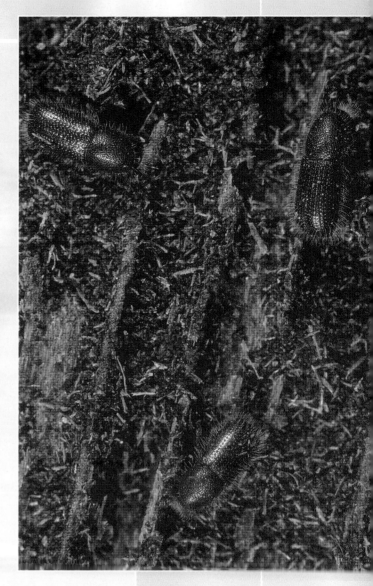

From beginning to end

We began this book with plant **germination** and have reached its conclusion with the death of a plant. To fuel the growth that takes them through life, plants make their food from the simplest ingredients imaginable. Yet using **energy** from the results of the incredible process of **photosynthesis**, plants can build themselves up to become complex living things, which continue growing throughout their lives, some of them developing into the largest, oldest and heaviest living things on the planet.

Try it yourself

Try these experiments to see for yourselves some of the plant processes you have learnt about in this book.

Tying up trees

You will need:

- A tree
- A plastic bag
- An elastic band or string

Choose a tree at school or home that has a branch you can reach, preferably in a shady spot. Early one evening, tie a small, clear plastic bag around the end of the branch, fitting in a good number of leaves. Tie the bag on tightly so that no air can escape.

Return to the tree next morning. In your bag there should be droplets of water. These are the result of **transpiration**. Warmth has heated the water in the leaves and changed it into the gas we call **water vapour**. Usually you cannot see this, but it has cooled again and gone back to being liquid water – forming the droplets you can see in your bag!

Keep a plant in the dark

This experiment shows you what happens when plants cannot get the light that they need to make food.

You will need:

- An area of grass, either at school or at home
- A waterproof box, such as an old washing-up bowl, which is opaque (you cannot see light through it)

This is simple. Place your box or bowl, upside-down, over a piece of grass. Leave it there for a week. When you return, take off the box or bowl and compare the grass that was beneath it with the rest of the lawn. The grass under the box will have turned pale and floppy. Without light, it has not been able to use the process of **photosynthesis** to produce food. If you left it without light for too much longer, it would die.

Play a trick on roots

Do **roots** always grow downwards? In this experiment you will try to trick a bean and see if you can change the direction in which its roots grow.

You will need:
- An old, transparent (see-through) drink bottle
- Blotting paper
- Water
- A broad bean **seed**

Carefully cut the top off the drink bottle so the top of it is flat. Take a piece of blotting paper and fold it so it will fit inside the bottle, wrapped around the inside. Wet it thoroughly before you put it inside. Slide your bean in between the paper and the bottle so that you can see it from the outside. Put the bottle somewhere warm. Check the bean after a few days. When a root begins to grow downwards, turn the bottle over, so the root looks like it is growing upwards. Leave the bottle for a few more days. What happens to the root?

The root should curl around so that it can continue to grow downwards. You can turn the bottle a second time and the same thing should happen. Remember, roots respond to the force of **gravity**, so they will always grow down, not up.

Setting off with seeds

Growing cress seeds is a great way to find out what seeds need to **germinate**.

You will need:
- Four small, shallow pots or trays (old margarine tubs will be fine)
- Cotton wool
- A packet of cress seeds
- Water

Put a thin layer of cotton wool in the bottom of all four trays. Pour water on the cotton wool in two of the trays only. Pour any excess water away so the cotton wool in these two trays is damp, not flooded.

Then sprinkle a thin layer of cress seeds on all four layers of cotton wool.

Next put one dry tray and one wet tray in a refrigerator. Put the other two trays somewhere warm and dark, such as an airing cupboard.

Check all four after a week. Which tray will hold the seeds that have started to grow, do you think? Seeds need warmth and moisture to begin to grow, so the seeds in damp cotton wool in the warm spot should be the ones that have started to sprout.

Looking at plant growth

A plant's life cycle

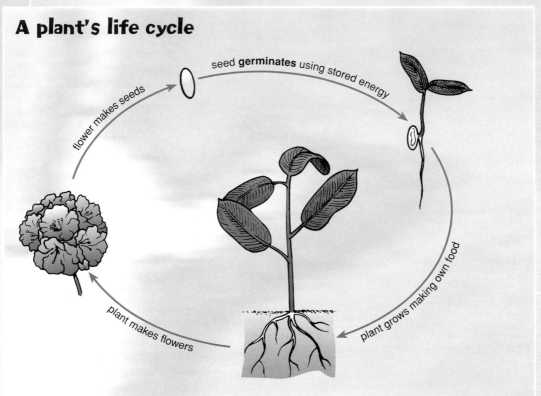

seed **germinates** using stored energy

flower makes seeds

plant grows making own food

plant makes flowers

Plants and growth cycles

Different plants have different growth cycles. **Annual** plants grow from **seed**, then flower, then spread seeds of their own and finally die, all in less than one year. **Biennial** plants take two years to complete their life cycle, flowering in the second year. **Perennial** plants, like trees and shrubs, live for two or more years, and most flower every year. Here are some of the plants that fall into these different categories.

Annual plants

Sunflower (*Helianthus*), African daisy (*Arctotis*), blazing star (*Bartonia*), marigold (*Calendula*), californian poppy (*Eschscholzia*), gazania (*Gazania*), heliotrope (*Heliotropium*), candytuft (*Iberis*), sweet pea (*Lathyrus*), statice (*Limonium*), flax (*Linum*), virginia stock (*Malcolmia*), livingstone daisy (*Mesembryanthemum*), poppy (*Papaver*), African marigold (*Tagetes*), black-eyed Susan (*Thunbergia*), nasturtium (*Tropaeolum*)

Biennial plants

Canterbury bell (*Campanula medium)*, wallflower (*Cheiranthus*), foxglove (*Digitalis purpurea*), honesty (*Lunaria*), forget-me-not (*Myosotis*), pansy (*Viola*), Sweet Williams (*Dianthus barbatus*), wild carrots

Perennial plants

African lily (*Agapanthus*), Japanese anemone (*Anemone*), columbine (*Aquilegia*), marsh marigold (*Calthia*), clematis (*Clematis*), pampas grass (*Cortaderia*), purple coneflower (*Echinacea*), globe thistle (*Echinops*), spurge (*Euphorbia*), sea holly (*Eryngium*), avens (*Geum*), plantain lily (*Hosta*), iris (*Iris*), lupin (*Lupinus*), maple (*Acer*), oak (*Quercus*), birch (*Betula*), redwood (*Sequoia*)

Transpiration and photosynthesis

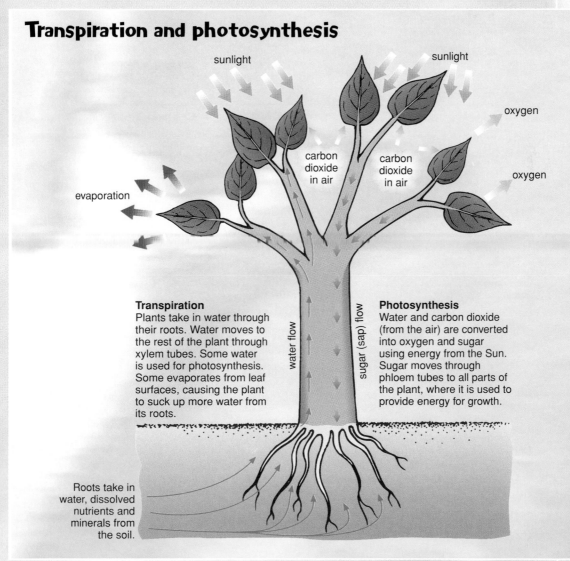

sunlight

sunlight

oxygen

carbon dioxide in air

carbon dioxide in air

oxygen

evaporation

Transpiration
Plants take in water through their roots. Water moves to the rest of the plant through xylem tubes. Some water is used for photosynthesis. Some evaporates from leaf surfaces, causing the plant to suck up more water from its roots.

water flow

sugar (sap) flow

Photosynthesis
Water and carbon dioxide (from the air) are converted into oxygen and sugar using energy from the Sun. Sugar moves through phloem tubes to all parts of the plant, where it is used to provide energy for growth.

Roots take in water, dissolved nutrients and minerals from the soil.

Glossary

algae plants that do not have leaves, stems or roots. Ferns are algae that have leaf-like fronds. Seaweed are algae that have holdfasts for anchorage instead of roots.

annual plant that grows, flowers, makes seeds and dies all within one year (or season)

annual rings rings you can see when the trunk of a tree is cut down. If you count annual rings, you can find out how old a tree is.

bacteria microscopic organisms that are found in the soil, water and air in all parts of the Earth. Bacteria are the oldest and simplest living things. Some bacteria can bring about decay in dead plants and animals.

biennial plant that lives for two years. It usually flowers, makes seeds and dies in the second year.

bud swelling on a plant stem of tiny, young, overlapping leaves or petals and other parts of a flower, ready to burst into bloom.

cabium layer of cells which are found between the xylem and phloem vessels in a plant

canopy uppermost layer of leafy branches in a forest

carbon dioxide gas in the air around us which plants use for photosynthesis

cells building blocks of living things, so small they can only be seen with a microscope. Some microbes consist of a single cell, but most plants and animals are made up of millions or billions of cells.

chlorophyll green pigment found in plants that is used in photosynthesis. Chlorophyll gives leaves their green colour.

chloroplasts tiny compartments within plant cells. Photosynthesis happens in a plant's chloroplasts.

coniferous kind of tree that bears its seeds in cones and has needle-like leaves

cork woody brown layer of dead cells found below the bark of a tree

cuticle waterproof layer covering the outside of a leaf

deciduous kind of tree that loses all its leaves in winter. In cool climates deciduous trees lose all their leaves before winter, but in tropical areas there are deciduous trees that lose all their leaves at the start of the dry season.

decompose rot away, by breaking down into smaller and smaller pieces

dissolve when something solid becomes a liquid

embryo a plant embryo is a very young plant contained in a seed

energy energy allows living things to do everything they need to live and grow. Plants and animals make the energy they need from their food.

epiphytes plants that grow on another plant for support, often to get themselves into a good position for receiving sunlight

evaporate when water turns from liquid into a vapour (an invisible gas). When clothes dry on a line, it is because the water evaporates and the vapour becomes part of the air.

fertilizer nutrient-rich powder or spray that plant-growers use to increase the amount or quality of their crop

fungi (singular is 'fungus') plant-like living things that do not make their food by photosynthesis and reproduce using spores. Mushrooms and toadstools are types of fungi.

germinate/germination when a seed starts to grow

gravity force that makes things drop when we let them go and that stops us floating off into space

grazing animal animal, such as rabbit or deer, that eat living plants such as grass or heather

habitat place in natural world where a particular organism lives

irrigation watering of land by farmers, using pumps, sprays or systems of canals and ditches, so that they can grow crops

minerals chemical building block of rocks. Plants need some minerals in order to grow and reproduce.

moss small green plant that grows in groups forming clumps and cushions close to the ground or rock on which they grow. Moss plants thrive in damp, shady habitats.

nectar sugary substance plants make to attract insects, which like to eat it

nutrients chemicals that plants and animals need in order to live

organisms living things, such as bacteria, cells, plants and animals

oxygen gas in the air; plants release oxygen into the air during the process of photosynthesis

parasite plant (or animal) that lives on and steals food from another living thing

peat bogs particular kind of marshy ground

perennial plant that lives for more than two years, often for many years

phloem tubes that carry food (sugars) made in the leaf to all the other parts of the plant

photosynthesis process by which plants make their own food using water, carbon dioxide (a gas in the air) and energy from sunlight

pigment natural substance that gives colour. Leaves are green because they contain a green pigment called chlorophyll.

respiration process by which living things release energy from their food

root plant part that grows underground and takes in water and nutrients

sap sugary liquid containing food made in the leaves. Sap flows in a plant's phloem tubes.

seed the part of a plant that contains the beginnings of a new plant

shoot plant part that grows out and up from a seed and on which a plant's first leaves grow

species kind of living thing

stem part of the plant that holds it upright and supports its leaves and flowers

stomata (singular is 'stoma') tiny openings on a leaf, usually on the underside, which let water vapour and oxygen out and carbon dioxide in

tendrils very long, thin leaves that wrap around supports to hold up a climbing plant

transpiration process by which water vapour is lost through the leaves of a plant

vascular plant plant that has xylem and phloem tubes for transporting water, nutrients and food to its various parts

water vapour moisture that is suspended as droplets in air, having changed from a liquid state into a gas, like steam from a kettle

waxy waterproof substance rather like plastic. Plants often have a very thin layer of natural wax around their leaves or fruit to stop these parts from drying out.

xylem tubes in a plant that carry water and nutrients from the roots to all the other parts of the plant